W9-AOZ-569

Susan Purviance and Marcia O'Shell

ALPHABET ANNIE ANNOUNCES AN
ALL-AMERICAN ALBUM

Illustrated by Ruth Brunner-Strosser

Houghton Mifflin Company
Boston 1988

To Ted, Conrad, and Chuckie, who taught me to share a good book with them.
S.P.

To Ann, Allison, David, and Wally, whose thrill of reading inspired me
to write this book so that others might have the same joy.
M.O.

Thanks to Bill, my husband, for his continual support and to David,
my son, for his creative contributions toward the betterment of this book.
R.B.S.

P. 50: The term Xerox is a registered trademark.

Library of Congress Cataloging-in-Publication Data

Purviance, Susan.
    Alphabet Annie announces an all-American album/Susan Purviance
and Marcia O'Shell; illustrated by Ruth Brunner-Strosser.
        p. cm.
    Summary: An alphabetical tour of characters performing various
activities in American cities, from Alice Allosaurus in Arizona City
to Zany Zelda Zebra in Zanesville.
    ISBN 0-395-48070-1
    1. English language—Alphabet—Juvenile literature.
[1. Alphabet.] I. O'Shell, Marcia. II. Brunner-Strosser, Ruth,
ill. III. Title.
PE1155.P87   1988   88-9214
[E]—dc19   CIP
                                      AC

Printed in the United States of America

Y   10   9   8   7   6   5   4   3   2   1

ALPHABET ANNIE ANNOUNCES AN
ALL-AMERICAN ALBUM

Alice Allosaurus admires
ancient artifacts in Arizona City.

Bobby Bear, a burly body builder,
builds better breakfasts in Battle Creek.

Charlie Chipmunk creates computer-controlled
contraptions for conventions in Chicago.

David Donkey dreams of
disco dancing in downtown Dover.

Egbert Eagle eagerly examines
every Easter egg in Erie.

Fat Fannie Fremont, formerly from Fairbanks,
flips flapjacks frantically on Frisco's freeways.

Gorgeous Gretta grazes while
Grover gets gasoline and grease in Great Bend.

Hilda the helpful hippo
holds high-strung hamsters in a Houston high-rise.

Ida Iverson imprints iron ingots
from Iron Mountain for interested industries.

Jason Jasper jumps joyfully
for jellybeans near Jacksonville.

Katie Karefree keeps kangaroos,
Kleenex, and ketchup kettles in her Kalamazoo kitchen.

Lucy the loser lost her luck,
loot, and luggage in Las Vegas.

Marna Mae makes macadamia muffins
on Maui and Molokai.

Nelly Namedropper noisily nibbles
numerous nachos near New York's newest nightclub.

Oliver Oceantide offers orange juice to
overheated old-timers in Orlando's orange groves.

Penelope the playful parrot
peddles pickles near a Pittsburgh pawnshop.

The Quincy quintuplets quibble
over quiche in Quaker Valley.

Rich Realtors rarely roller-skate
between Raleigh and Richmond.

Susie Strauss skis, sings, and
strums on the slopes of Sun Valley.

Trudy Turtle travels on
the turnpike toward Toledo.

Uncle Ulysses unfolds umbrellas
in University Park.

Vickie Viper vacations in
Vancouver and visits volcanoes.

Wilbur Walrus wants to work
with wringer washers in Walla Walla, Washington.

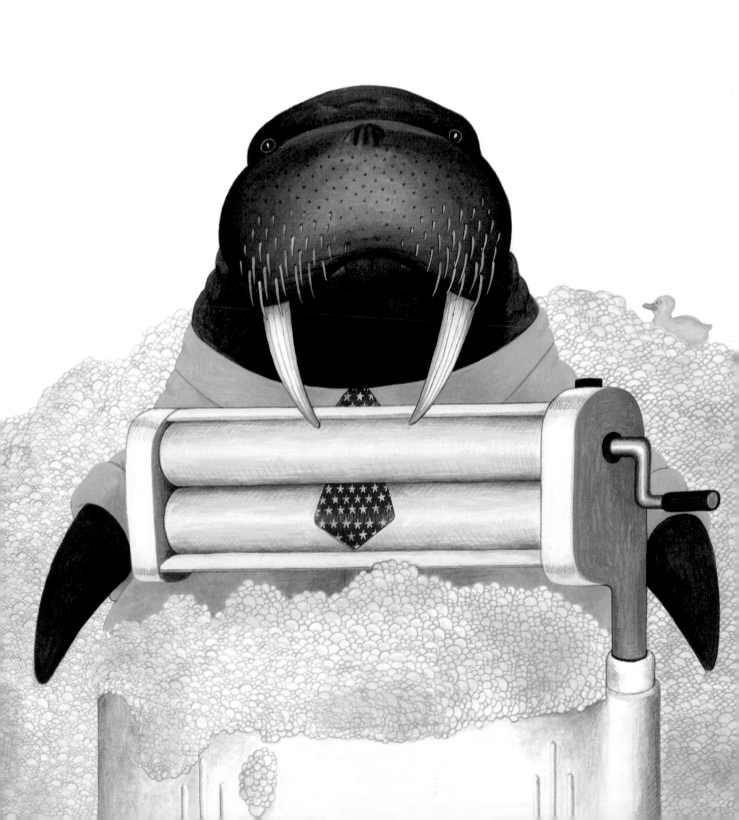

Xavier Xeroxes x-rays in Xenia.

Young Yedda Yak yodels
for yummy yogurt in Yakima.

Zany Zelda Zebra zigzags
zippers in Zanesville.